Racial Segregation

Plessy v. Ferguson

ZACHARY DEIBEL

Cavendish
Square
New York

Published in 2019 by Cavendish Square Publishing, LLC
243 5th Avenue, Suite 136, New York, NY 10016

Cataloging-in-Publication Data

Names: Deibel, Zachary.
Title: Racial segregation: Plessy v. Ferguson / Zachary Deibel.
Description: First edition. | New York : Cavendish Square, 2019. |
Series: Courting history | Includes glossary and index.
Identifiers: ISBN 9781502635914 (pbk.) | ISBN 9781502635891
(library bound) | ISBN 9781502635907 (ebook)
Subjects: LCSH: Plessy, Homer Adolph--Trials, litigation, etc.--Juvenile literature.
| Segregation in transportation--Law and legislation--Louisiana--
History--Juvenile literature. | Segregation--Law and legislation--United
States--History--Juvenile literature. | African Americans--Civil rights--
History. | United States--Race relations--History--Juvenile literature.
Classification: LCC KF223.P56 D45 2019 | DDC 342.7308'73--dc23

Editorial Director: David McNamara
Editor: Chet'la Sebree
Copy Editor: Nathan Heidelberger
Associate Art Director: Amy Greenan
Designer: Joe Parenteau
Production Coordinator: Karol Szymczuk
Photo Research: J8 Media

Printed in the United States of America

Contents

ONE
Reconstruction and Inequality

On July 19, 1890, an article appeared in the *Crusader*, an African American publication based in New Orleans, Louisiana. The *Crusader* article called Louisiana's black population to action. The state had just passed the Separate Car Act of 1890. The act provided "equal but separate accommodations for the white and colored races." In other words, white passengers and African American passengers would have to ride in separate train cars. The article was written by author and activist Rodolphe Desdunes. In the piece, he argued that African Americans "have largely patronized the railroads ... They can withdraw the patronage from these corporations and travel only by necessity." He was suggesting that African Americans no longer take the trains if they were required to ride in separate cars.

Desdunes was a member of the Comité des Citoyens, or Citizens' Committee. It was a civil rights organization of black, white, and Creole people in Louisiana. The *Crusader* published articles by the members of the organization. Through the newspaper, Desdunes and the Comité organized a boycott, or a protest in which protesters stop using a service, of the Louisiana rail system. Eventually, Comité member Homer Adolph Plessy would put the Separate Car Act to the test.

Plessy was born in New Orleans in 1862. He was born to a family that fled Haiti during a slave rebellion. His family was

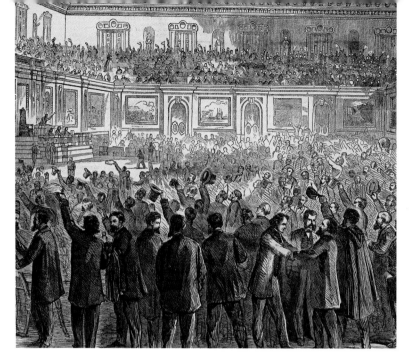

This 1865 illustration shows the reaction in the House of Representatives after the passage of the Thirteenth Amendment, which abolished slavery.

from both France and Haiti. His family was made up of both white Europeans and free black Haitians. When Plessy was young, black people enjoyed a fair amount of freedom and citizenship in New Orleans. They were allowed to do things like ride on trains without having to use separate cars. Things started to change as Plessy got older. Laws like the Separate Car Act were created.

To most people, Plessy looked like a white man. However, he was legally considered a person of color because he was one-eighth black. This put Plessy in a unique position when it came to the Separate Car Act. He was able to board the white passenger car without anyone noticing that he was black. Plessy did just that. He intentionally boarded a white-only East Louisiana Railroad car. He then informed one of the officials that he was a person of color. This action launched a national debate over the constitutionality of segregation, or the legal separation of people based on race.

5

The United States Supreme Court's decision in this case would have long-lasting effects.

Reconstruction and Attempts to Enforce Equality

The United States Civil War lasted from April 12, 1861, to May 13, 1865. It started because, between 1860 and 1861, eleven of the thirty-four states announced their intention to become their own country, the Confederate States of America. The Confederates had many reasons for wanting to be a separate country. The primary reason involved the institution of slavery. Slavery was a big part of the social and economic culture in the confederacy.

In January 1865, the Thirteenth Amendment to the Constitution was passed. This amendment abolished, or put an end to, slavery and involuntary servitude across the nation. The Civil War ended a few months after this amendment was passed. After the war, there were many other changes to the country's laws. The majority of lawmakers in Congress were Republicans like President Abraham Lincoln. There was a group within the Republican Party known as Radical Republicans. They began to pass laws based on their firm support of equality for African Americans. These laws aimed to prevent states from violating the rights of African Americans. The group was considered "radical" because many white Americans did not believe that African Americans should be treated equally.

These Republicans were responsible for passing the Reconstruction Amendments. These are the Thirteenth, Fourteenth, and Fifteenth Amendments to the US Constitution. They were passed between 1865 and 1870.

Although the Thirteenth Amendment abolished slavery, more amendments were needed to protect the rights of newly freed African Americans.

In 1866, Congress passed the Civil Rights Act of 1866, which aimed to protect African Americans from legal

A Segregated Nation

As early as 1865, states began passing laws that segregated public spaces. These laws aimed to limit opportunities for African Americans. Mississippi banned freed slaves from renting land to farm. This forced many workers into farming contracts that often limited their rights. In 1870, Virginia made black and white children attend separate schools. Southern states also started to create new state constitutions between 1890 and 1908. These constitutions limited voting rights for African Americans.

Even in Northern states, segregation existed. It was not necessarily legal segregation. The segregation in the North was organized within communities. For instance, Harlem became a mostly African American community in New York City. Local officials forced black migrants into the neighborhood, while other neighborhoods remained largely white.

Segregation also often went with racial violence against blacks throughout the country. Northern and Southern states alike reported thousands of murders of African Americans throughout the Reconstruction Era.

violations of their liberties. The act provided citizenship
to all people born in the United States. It also guaranteed
those people the same rights "as [are] enjoyed by white
citizens." In other words, all citizens were to be treated
equally by the law regardless of their race. This law gave
power to the Thirteenth Amendment. It established a clear
expectation that the Southern states would treat free African
Americans equally.

Vice President Andrew Johnson became president after
Lincoln's assassination, or murder for political reasons. He
was a Democrat, and he did not like the Civil Rights Act
of 1866. He believed the law was unconstitutional. On
March 27, 1866, Johnson wrote that he was going to veto, or
reject, the act. Johnson feared it would renew "the spirit of
rebellion" among white Southerners. In other words, he feared
that white Southerners would develop the same feelings that
led to the Civil War.

Despite Johnson's concerns, the law was passed. It was
important to the Republicans' mission of rebuilding a
nation around equality. However, they were not finished.
They wanted to protect the rights of all citizens. In 1866,
Congress approved the Fourteenth Amendment to the US
Constitution. It was ratified, or made official, in 1868.

The Fourteenth Amendment is a significant addition
to the Constitution. There are several sections to the
amendment. The first section has remained important to
understanding the rights and liberties of American citizens.
It states:

> All persons born or naturalized in the United States,
> and subject to the jurisdiction thereof, are citizens of
> the United States and of the State wherein they reside.

No State shall make or enforce any law which shall abridge the privileges or immunities of citizens of the United States; nor shall any State deprive any person of life, liberty, or property, without due process of law; nor deny to any person within its jurisdiction the equal protection of the laws.

The Fourteenth Amendment (pictured here) sought to protect the freedoms of all Americans.

Racial Segregation:
Plessy v. Ferguson

This single section contains four major legal concepts. First, it establishes that all people born in the United States are citizens. It also gives rights to naturalized citizens, or people who go through a legal process to become US citizens. All US citizens are citizens of both the nation and the state in which they live. These citizens are also subject to the laws of both the nation and the individual state.

Second, this section established that individual states cannot violate individuals' "privileges or immunities." This second part is known as the privileges or immunities clause. It means that a state cannot create or enforce laws that violate an individual's constitutional rights.

Third, a state cannot take away individuals' privileges or immunities without a fair trial. This portion is known as the due process clause. It gives all citizens the right to fair treatment by the judicial system.

Finally, a state cannot pass laws that aim to treat citizens or protect their rights differently. This final part guarantees all citizens equal treatment under the laws. It is known as the equal protection clause. In total, the Fourteenth Amendment aimed to prevent the states from taking away the rights of African Americans. It also aimed to make sure African Americans were treated the same as white citizens by law.

A few years later, in 1869, Congress passed the Fifteenth Amendment to the US Constitution. This amendment was intended to expand on the mission of the Fourteenth Amendment. It gives all male citizens the right to vote. It was created so that neither the state nor the federal government could keep someone from voting based on his or her race.

The Fifteenth Amendment secured voting rights for African American men.

The Reconstruction Amendments were attempts to protect the rights of freed slaves. In 1875, Congress went even further. It passed another Civil Rights Act. The act aimed to enforce these previous amendments more. The law stated that people of all races could enjoy public spaces equally. The act was significant and controversial. It aimed to protect the rights of freed slaves and African Americans in all aspects of life. However, many Americans worried these acts would lead to more violence.

Deconstructing Reconstruction

African American lawmakers were central to these acts and amendments. Throughout the 1860s and 1870s, many black candidates were elected to positions in state and local governments. These lawmakers aimed to protect the newly freed populations. Hiram Revels and Blanche Bruce were both elected to the United States Senate from Mississippi, in 1870 and 1874, respectively. Both men were African Americans. Between 1869 and 1901, twenty-two black congressmen were elected from the former Confederate states. In total, over six hundred African Americans were elected to public office at the state and national levels. However, white people in the South began battling to regain control of local, state, and national politics.

By the end of 1901, there were no African Americans serving in Congress. Slowly, states found ways to stop supporting progress toward equality. Many people did not believe racial equality was necessary or productive. The South tended to refuse African Americans equality. The rest of the nation tended to not help to enforce laws about equality. However, those affected by such treatment refused to stay silent. Many stood up to oppose this injustice. These people included the activists who published the New Orleans *Crusader*. These people also included a young public education activist named Homer Plessy.

15,248.

Supreme Court of the United States,

No. 210 , October Term, 1895.

Homer Adolph Plessy
Plaintiff in Error,

vs.

J. H. Ferguson, Judge of Section "A"
Criminal District Court for the Parish
of Orleans.

In Error to the Supreme Court of the State of
Louisiana

This cause came on to be heard on the transcript of the
record from the Supreme Court of the State of Louisiana,
and was argued by counsel.

On consideration whereof, It is now here ordered and
adjudged by this Court that the judgment of the said Supreme
Court, in this cause, be, and the same is hereby, affirmed
with costs.

Per Mr. Justice Brown,
May 18, 1896.

Dissenting:
Mr. Justice Harlan

Homer Plessy petitioned the Supreme Court to rule on the issue
of segregation.

TWO
Segregation and the Law

In 1883, the Supreme Court decided that the Civil Rights Act of 1875 was unconstitutional. This decision was made in the *Civil Rights Cases*. Justice Joseph Bradley wrote that the Fourteenth Amendment only prevented the government from discriminating. It did not keep private citizens or organizations from discriminating.

Bradley claimed that the Civil Rights Acts also violated the original purpose of the Fourteenth Amendment. The amendment did not exist to stop the states from discriminating on the basis of race. Instead, it only existed to provide citizenship and its privileges to freed slaves. Not all justices on the court agreed with Bradley, however.

Justice John Marshall Harlan disagreed. He thought that the Thirteenth Amendment was responsible for more than abolishing slavery. He believed it was created to protect the freedoms of the newly freed African Americans. In Harlan's view, it made sense to pass laws like the Civil Rights Act. It was only through such laws that the government could prevent states from treating former slaves as second-class citizens. Harlan believed that the Reconstruction Amendments were responsible for more than protecting former slaves from slavery. The laws existed to protect freed slaves from discrimination on the basis of race.

Many editorial cartoons criticized segregation. This one features caricatures of African Americans.

Segregating a Nation

Harlan's opinion, or written legal statement about a decision, was not a popular one. Black codes were introduced throughout the South after the 1883 decision. The laws controlled nearly every aspect of African Americans' lives. These laws prevented African Americans from having the same freedoms as white Americans.

In 1898, Louisiana revised its state constitution. The new constitution required a person to be both literate, or able to read, and a property owner to vote. Many African Americans in the South had not received an education. For that reason, many could not read. Also, many African Americans were tenant farmers or sharecroppers, people who pay their rent with crops they grow. In other words, they did not own land. For these reasons, the new Louisiana constitution made it almost impossible for African Americans to vote.

15

Many of the black codes did not just deny opportunities to blacks. They also actively separated African Americans from white society. For instance, one Mississippi code stated that "it shall not be lawful for any freedman … to intermarry with any white person." In other words, it was illegal for a formerly

Congress and the President Remain Silent

In 1896, when *Plessy v. Ferguson* came before the Supreme Court, Congress contained many members who both opposed and supported segregation. Republicans controlled both the Senate and the House of Representatives. President Grover Cleveland, a Democrat, supported the *Plessy* decision as a victory for states' rights to make decisions about segregation.

Despite the fact that the case is remembered as important, little attention was paid to the ruling in 1896. Political leaders of both parties almost completely ignored the case on the campaign trail during that year's election season. Newspapers like the *Roanoke Daily Times* in Virginia and the *New Ulm Review* in Minnesota published short articles on the court's decision. Neither of those articles was more than two or three paragraphs. The fact that few cared about the decision was different from Republicans' vision of Reconstruction. People seemed to be OK with the unequal treatment of African Americans.

enslaved person to marry a white person. These laws were also used to control the ways in which African Americans used public facilities. For instance, Tennessee passed twenty different laws that segregated railroads, schools, public resources, and other facilities.

Activists Respond

Many states were passing laws segregating African Americans. However, the federal government had not offered an opinion on it yet because no one had challenged segregation as a violation of African Americans' rights. Homer Plessy, Rodolphe Desdunes, and the Comité des Citoyens in New Orleans hoped to change that.

On June 7, 1892, Plessy purchased a train ticket from New Orleans to Covington, Louisiana. He bought a ticket to the white-only passenger car. The Comité and its members notified police that Plessy did this. Plessy and the Comité did not want Plessy to get away with breaking a law. In fact, Plessy wanted to be arrested. After his arrest, the organization declared it would challenge Louisiana's Separate Car Act. This act required that train cars be segregated based on race. The Comité wanted to challenge the act as a violation of the Thirteenth and Fourteenth Amendments.

Homer Plessy's trial began on October 13, 1892. The Comité did not plan to win. Plessy had clearly violated the Separate Car Act. Instead, the group believed the case needed to reach the federal courts. They believed the US Supreme Court would not support segregation like the Southern courts would. In the local court, Judge John H. Ferguson found Plessy guilty of having violated the law. He also found him guilty of refusing to obey when he was asked to

Racial Segregation:
Plessy v. Ferguson

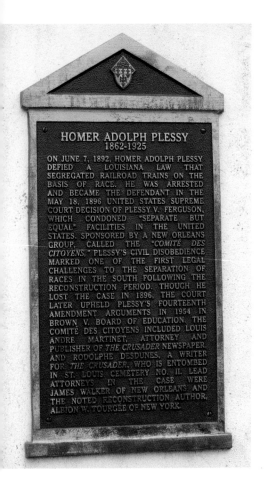

This plaque marks the tomb of Homer Plessy, an activist for African American rights who challenged the constitutionality of segregation.

leave the white car. Plessy appealed to the Louisiana Supreme Court, meaning he asked the higher court to reconsider Ferguson's decision. By doing so, Plessy was filing suit against the state and Ferguson himself. He argued that both Ferguson's decision and the state's law had violated his constitutional rights.

Plessy believed the state had violated his right to equal protection and due process. In other words, Plessy thought that the state had failed to give him the same privileges and rights as other citizens. It failed to do this because it did not allow him to ride in the white cars. This was a violation of the equal protection clause. Plessy also thought that the state had failed to give him fair treatment, or due process, under the law. Both of these rights were protected by the Fourteenth Amendment.

Plessy's attorneys felt that more laws had been violated. His legal team was led by the civil rights activist Albion Tourgée. Tourgée argued that Plessy's Thirteenth

Amendment rights had also been violated. The Thirteenth Amendment secured each American citizen the right to be free from slavery. Tourgée argued that segregation created a near-slave society for African Americans.

At the time, the assistant district attorney for New Orleans was Lionel Adams. He was an experienced politician and lawyer. He defended the law and Plessy's conviction to the Louisiana Supreme Court. Adams argued the law was within the state's police powers. He argued that the state

The leader of Plessy's legal team, Albion Tourgée, had a long political and professional history of challenging discrimination and segregation.

19

had the right to protect its own citizens. This right had been given to the states by the Tenth Amendment to the United States Constitution. The Tenth Amendment left all powers not listed in the Constitution up to the states or to the people. Adams argued that the state had the power to segregate if the segregation was meant to protect its people. He stated that it was not an act of discrimination. It was an act of protection. He also claimed whites were forbidden from entering black cars, just as blacks were forbidden from entering white cars.

Ultimately, the Louisiana Supreme Court sided with Adams. The law had not violated the state's or the country's constitutions because it affected all races equally. The court stated that the Separate Car Act was legal so long as the railroad company provided equal train accommodations for both white and black passengers.

Plessy and his lawyers were not satisfied with this decision. They decided to appeal the Louisiana Supreme Court's decision to the United States Supreme Court.

The US Supreme Court does not hear every case that is submitted to it for appeal. A case needs a writ of certiorari, or an official acceptance, from the Supreme Court for the court to hear the case. In general, the US Supreme Court only hears cases that call the Constitution into question. In other words, the US Supreme Court makes decisions in cases where it is deciding whether or not someone's constitutional rights have been violated. It may also choose to hear a case that questions the way we understand the Constitution. In *Plessy v. Ferguson*, Plessy's attorneys filed for a writ of certiorari. One was granted by the court. It agreed to hear the case.

IN THE SUPREME COURT OF THE UNITED STATES.

HOMER ADOLPH PLESSY, Plaintiff in Error,
vs.
J. H. FERGUSON, Judge of Section "A" Criminal District Court for the Parish of New Orleans.

———

Error to the Supreme Court of Louisiana.

———

Brief for Plaintiff in Error.

STATEMENT OF CASE.

The Plaintiff in Error was arrested on the affidavit of two witnesses charging him with violation of Act No. 111, of the Laws of Louisiana, session of 1890, averring that he was "a colored passenger on a train of the East Louisiana Railroad Company," who did "insist upon going into and remaining in a compartment of a coach of said train which had been assigned to white passengers." (See pp 4-5 of printed record.)

On this affidavit, a warrant issued and he was brought before A. R. Moulin, Recorder, by whom, examination being waived, he was bound over to section A of the Criminal Court of the Parish of New Orleans, giving bond in the sum of $500 for his appearance to answer said charge. (Printed Record, p. 5.)

On the 22d November, 1892, an information was duly filed in said Court based on said proceedings before said Recorder, charging said Plessy with violation of said statute, 111, Acts of 1890, of the State of Louisiana. (See pages 5-6 of printed record.)

To this information, the said Plessy upon arraignment, filed a plea in bar of the jurisdiction of the Court, based on the averment that said Act, No. 111, of 1890, was null and void, being in conflict with the Constitution of the United States. (Printed Record, pp 8-10 and 16-18.)

To this plea the District Attorney demurred. (Printed Record pp. 18-19.) And on this the defendant joined issue. (Printed Record p. 19.) On the issue joined, respondent in error, the Judge of said Court, over-ruled the plea of the defendant Plessy and ordered that he plead over to said presentment. (Printed Record pp. 19-23.)

Thereupon, the said Plessy, by his counsel made application to the Supreme Court of the State of Louisiana for a writ of Prohibition and Certiorari, based upon his plea in the court below. On the hearing, the

Tourgée and his team submitted this lengthy brief to sway the court to rule against the Separate Car Act, a clear violation of black citizens' rights.

Tourgée and Plessy were not optimistic about their odds of winning. They believed that many of the Supreme Court justices did not support their argument.

The Supreme Court is made up of nine justices. There are eight associate justices and one chief justice. The chief justice manages and oversees the other eight justices. At the time of *Plessy v. Ferguson*, eight of the nine justices had narrow views of the Fourteenth Amendment. These narrow views did not support the arguments Tourgée and Plessy were making. Even still, Plessy's legal team would argue that the nation should uphold the promise made in the Declaration of Independence. Plessy's team asked the court to follow the belief that "all men are created equal."

THREE

Arguing Before the Court

Soldier, lawyer, and civil rights activist Albion Tourgée served as Homer Plessy's lead attorney. He also asked for the help of Samuel F. Phillips. Phillips was an experienced attorney and political figure. He had served under Ulysses S. Grant and three other presidents as solicitor general. The solicitor general is responsible for arguing cases before the Supreme Court on behalf of the US government. As solicitor general, Phillips had argued in favor of the Civil Rights Act of 1875 before the Supreme Court in 1883. F. D. McKenney and James C. Walker helped Phillips and Tourgée as well.

Plessy's Attorneys Brief the Court

Phillips and McKenney filed a brief, or legal summary, that included several arguments. Phillips explained the story behind the case. Plessy had respectfully disobeyed the law. Despite Plessy's politeness, the railroad official was legally required to enforce the segregation of the cars. Phillips argued that the law itself was a violation of the Fourteenth Amendment. It violated Plessy's right to the privileges and immunities of American citizenship. The act also did not give him equal protection under the law compared to white citizens.

PLESSY V. FERGUSON
PRESS STREET RAILROAD YARDS
Site of the Arrest of Homer Adolph Plessy
(Continued from other side)

• • •

Homer Plessy was born Homère Patris Plessy on March 17, 1863 in New Orleans. His parents were carpenter (Joseph) Adolphe Plessy and seamstress Rosa Debergue, both classified as people of color. Homer Plessy died on March 1, 1925. He is entombed in St. Louis Cemetery No. 1.
John Howard Ferguson was born in 1838 in Martha's Vineyard, MA. He was appointed Judge in Section A of the Orleans Parish Criminal Court in 1892 and ruled against Plessy in November of the same year. He is buried in Lafayette Cemetery.

MEMBERS OF THE CITIZENS' COMMITTEE (1891-1896)

Arthur Esteves, President; C. C. Antoine, Vice-President; Firmin Christophe, Secretary; G. G. Johnson, Asst. Secretary; Paul Bonseigneur, Treasurer; Laurent Auguste; Rudolph B. Baquie; Rodolphe L. Desdunes; A. J. Giuranovich; Alcee Labat; E. A. Williams; Pierre Chevalier; Louis A. Martinet; Numa E. Mansion; L. J. Joubert; A. B. Kennedy; Myrthil J. Piron; Eugene Luscy; Julius Hall; Frank Hall; Noel Bachus; George Geddes; A. E. P. Albert.

CRESCENT CITY PEACE ALLIANCE

This marker stands in New Orleans at the Press Street Railroad Yard, where Plessy disobeyed the Separate Car Act.

Phillips also claimed the law was in violation of the Thirteenth Amendment. He argued that segregation created its own form of slavery. Segregation suggested that a passenger was either a superior or inferior class of citizen based on his or her race. It reduced freedom for those who were considered to be part of the lower class. In Phillips's view, this reduced freedom and lower-class status looked a lot like slavery.

Tourgée and Walker also wrote a brief. It focused on similar issues as Phillips and McKenney's, but it also expanded on others. Tourgée argued that the Separate Car Act "imposed a badge of servitude." In other words, the law treated African Americans like lower-class citizens. He also argued that the law continued "the distinction of race and caste," or class, that the Thirteenth Amendment aimed to erase. Tourgée stated that segregation created the race-based distinctions that slave states used. He believed segregation had permanent effects, like slavery, on the lives of African Americans. For these reasons, Tourgée felt the Separate Car Act was in violation of the Thirteenth Amendment.

Throughout the South, segregated facilities like this all-black school provided unequal resources to people of color.

Racial Segregation:
Plessy v. Ferguson

The key argument for Plessy's legal team was that the Fourteenth Amendment guaranteed Plessy citizenship. His rights as a citizen were being violated by Louisiana's race-based laws. In order for a state to violate a citizen's rights, it must prove it has a reasonable cause to do so. Tourgée argued that the Separate Car Act was unreasonable.

Tourgée's argument did not stop with these two amendments. He also argued that Plessy had been denied his whiteness and, more important, his citizenship. Tourgée believed that Plessy should be allowed to call himself white because he was seven-eighths white. He was only one-eighth African American. His skin made him seem white. However, according to the Separate Car Act, Plessy was legally black. Tourgée stated that it was difficult to accurately label anyone on the basis of race. Tourgée also discussed the imbalanced treatment of black people. He argued that "most white persons if given a choice, would prefer death to life in the United States as colored persons." He pointed out how aware white people were of this imbalance.

Additionally, Tourgée argued that Plessy's rights were more important than any law of the state of Louisiana. Both the Fourteenth Amendment and Article IV of the Constitution forbade the states from interfering with the rights of an American citizen. The Supreme Court had the opportunity to protect Plessy from the state violating his rights. Tourgée encouraged the court to do so. He claimed that the state did not have a reasonable enough justification for the Separate Car Act. He asked the court to protect Plessy's constitutional rights.

At the end of the brief, Tourgée asked the justices to consider an imaginary situation. If they woke up one morning

These nine Supreme Court justices oversaw the *Plessy v. Ferguson* case.

with "black skin and curly hair," would they still interpret the Fourteenth Amendment the same way? If they were black, would they suggest that such laws were reasonable? Would they believe segregation was a fair state action?

27

A Lawyer and an Activist

Albion Tourgée was a passionate Republican and an opponent of slavery. He served in the Union army during the Civil War. After he served in the war, he eventually moved to Greensboro, North Carolina. He began a career as an editor of a Republican newspaper. Within a few years, he was elected to serve as a judge in North Carolina. He continued his advocacy for racial equality during and after his judgeship. He also founded the National Citizens' Rights Association in 1891.

In 1896, he represented Homer Plessy in front of the Supreme Court. He argued that segregation violated the concept of "blind justice." In other words, justice should apply to everyone regardless of who they are. Tourgée argued segregation established an unconstitutional caste system. In a brief to the court, Tourgée wrote, "Justice is pictured as blind, and her daughter, the Law, ought at least to be color-blind." In other words, the law should apply to all people equally, regardless of the color of their skin. Although he was unsuccessful at winning the case, Tourgée argued for the same principles he had advocated his entire life. He believed in equality under the law and justice for all, regardless of race.

The State Responds

The state needed to defend the Separate Car Act as a reasonable law. It needed to prove that it did not violate the Constitution. It also needed to show that Louisiana's state government was allowed to make its own decisions about segregation. The briefs submitted by the state of Louisiana defended the law by relying on similar arguments as those made in lower courts.

Milton J. Cunningham, the attorney general of Louisiana, defended the state and Judge Ferguson in the US Supreme Court case. For his defense, he simply resubmitted the written opinion of Justice Charles Fenner from when the case was decided in the Louisiana Supreme Court. Cunningham believed that Fenner had "thoroughly covered the grounds presented in the case." In other words, Cunningham did not feel like he had a lot to add to Fenner's opinion.

The justice's opinion stated that Plessy had no grounds to sue under the Thirteenth Amendment. Fenner mentioned the 1883 *Civil Rights Cases* decision. He said that the Supreme Court's ruling in 1883 concluded that laws about segregation did not create "any badge of slavery." In other words, segregation could not legally be equated with slavery. Fenner also argued that the Fourteenth Amendment did not apply here in Plessy's case. The state had not denied Plessy rights or privileges. The state had simply required he enjoy these rights and privileges in a certain way. White and black passengers faced the same law. Since they faced the same law, there was no lack of equal treatment.

There was one thing Cunningham added to Fenner's argument. Cunningham reminded the court that the state had the power to create its own laws about segregation. The

Justice Charles Fenner ruled against Plessy at the state level.

Tenth Amendment to the US Constitution gave each state the power to decide what was best for its citizens.

Cunningham was not arguing the case for the state and Ferguson alone. He worked with Washington lawyer Alexander Porter Morse. He also worked with Lionel Adams, the New Orleans assistant district attorney. Adams had been the state's lawyer against Plessy when the case went to the Louisiana Supreme Court.

Together, the three men developed a brief. In the brief, they focused on existing precedent, or examples from previous cases, to make their case. They argued that states had very few limits on what types of laws they could enforce. They cited several cases and laws. They argued that the segregation of public facilities was common in many states. They argued that the Supreme Court had ruled in favor of segregation laws in the past.

They even mentioned a case that ruled against segregation. *Strauder v. West Virginia* (1880) was an exception to the Supreme Court's tendency to rule in favor of segregation. In that case, the Supreme Court ruled that it was unconstitutional to exclude African Americans from juries. The right to be part of the legal process was protected by the Constitution. Any law that excluded African Americans from being a part of the legal process was indeed unconstitutional. The lawyers agreed with this because the right to be a part of the legal process is a federally protected right. Morse argued that the right to ride a streetcar in Louisiana in a certain way was not a federally protected right.

Morse also made an argument about federally protected states' rights. He argued that the Supreme Court deciding that any act of segregation by a state government was unconstitutional would be an unnecessary involvement of the federal government in state politics. It violated the states' rights outlined in the Tenth Amendment. Morse argued that no national liberty had been taken away by Louisiana's Separate

The Cabildo on Jackson Square in New Orleans housed the Louisiana Supreme Court at the time of Plessy's case.

Car Act. For that reason, he believed that the Supreme Court had no power to declare the act unconstitutional.

The lawyers also made a point that it was reasonable to separate the races. They argued that the state was acting in its citizens' best interest. Morse stated that there was "the danger of friction from too intimate contact" between races. In other words, both races sitting in the same car could lead to bad things like violence. He thought this threat of "friction" was enough of a reason for the state to segregate cars.

The state argued that segregation of rail cars and drinking fountains was legal so long as it provided equal accommodations to both parties.

The brief also argued that Plessy's race was unrelated to the case. Regardless of whether Plessy was white or black, he would have been arrested if he boarded the wrong car and refused to move. They argued that the law applied to all races equally.

Segregation Before the Court

No records survive of the actual oral arguments in *Plessy v. Ferguson*. The briefs filed by both sides provide an outline of what was offered to the justices. Some of Tourgée's notes prepared before his appearance in front of the Supreme Court remain. Primarily, his notes point out the dangers of the government making decisions based on race. He looked at the problems that affected other minorities, like Jewish populations in Europe. He believed that segregation went against the spirit of the Declaration of Independence. He thought all people, regardless of race, should share the same rights, liberties, and protections. Unfortunately, whatever arguments Tourgée made in court were unsuccessful.

FOUR

The Ruling of the Court

On May 18, 1896, the Supreme Court of the United States made a decision on *Plessy v. Ferguson*. A Louisiana newspaper called the *Weekly Messenger* reported on the ruling on May 19. It wrote that the Supreme Court had decided that the Separate Car Act was constitutional.

The Supreme Court had sided with the state in a 7–1 decision. One justice did not vote. The court believed that segregation of train cars was legal as long as equal accommodations were provided for both sets of passengers. If the accommodations were equal, then the law was not in violation of the Fourteenth Amendment. Although the decision was specifically about train cars, the ruling would establish a precedent for other types of segregation. This precedent would be called the "separate but equal" doctrine. A doctrine is an established government policy. The "separate but equal" doctrine would be used as validation for segregating other facilities in years to come.

The *Weekly Messenger* recognized the effects of this decision. The article stated that the decision had removed the hope that African Americans could "mix freely" with white Americans. According to the paper, the decision saved white

This drawing depicts an African American being dismissed from a whites-only train car.

people "much discomfort and irritation … as they travel in Louisiana." In other words, white people would not have to be "bothered" by interacting with African Americans. The article also stated that the decision had established "the principle of the 'Jim Crow' car." "Jim Crow" was an insulting term used to describe African Americans.

Bills like this one allowed railroad companies to control all aspects of transportation in the Confederacy during the Civil War.

The Majority Rules

Justice Henry Billings Brown wrote the majority opinion, or written decision that the majority of the justices agreed with. Justices Melville Fuller, Stephen Johnson Field, Horace Gray, George Shiras, Edward Douglass White, and Rufus Peckham sided with him. The opinion aimed to answer the constitutional question raised. First, did Louisiana's law violate the Thirteenth Amendment by treating African Americans as second-class citizens? Second, did the act violate citizens' rights under the equal protection clause or the privileges and immunities clause of the Fourteenth Amendment?

To both questions, the majority of the court answered "no." In the opinion, Brown wrote "that it [the Separate Car Act] does not conflict with the Thirteenth Amendment." In the majority's view, slavery was defined as "involuntary servitude." It did not define slavery as second-class citizenship. The opinion mentioned the *Civil Rights Cases* (1883) and the

Chief Justice Fuller's legal philosophy guided the court.

Slaughterhouse Cases (1873). It used these cases to argue that the Thirteenth Amendment existed only to end the institution of slavery. The majority of the justices did not believe the Separate Car Act was an attempt to "reestablish a state of involuntary servitude." For that reason, they believed the act did not violate the Thirteenth Amendment. This narrow view of the Constitution was the basis of the whole opinion.

Brown then turned his attention to the Fourteenth Amendment. He detailed the court's previous understanding of this amendment as well. Brown argued that the *Slaughterhouse Cases* confirmed that the Fourteenth Amendment's "main purpose was to establish the citizenship of the negro … and to protect … the privileges and immunities of citizens of the United States." In other words, the amendment existed to make African Americans citizens and to protect their rights as citizens. He did not believe the law was "intended to abolish distinctions based upon color." He meant that he did not think the law was created to end social discrimination. Brown believed the Fourteenth Amendment only protected citizens' equality under the law, not their equality within society. In this way, it was OK to socially treat people of different races differently as long as both were equally protected under the law. In

Brown's eyes, the Separate Car Act did not provide unequal protection to African Americans. In fact, it did the exact opposite. It provided equal cars. These cars were just separate ones for people of different backgrounds.

In fact, Brown believed Louisiana was acting in its citizens' best interests. He wrote that segregation laws are reasonable if they "are enacted in good faith for the promotion for the public good, and not for the annoyance or oppression of a particular class." In other words, he thought the law was protecting the citizens. He did not believe the law was meant to keep African Americans down. For these reasons, Brown believed the Separate Car Act was reasonable. The act did not deny a service or access to a law to any of Louisiana's citizens. The state was simply trying to accommodate citizens of different races. Brown stated that it was not the law's fault if one race understood this separate service to be a "badge of inferiority."

Justice Brown wrote the majority opinion explaining the decision.

Brown also thought that changing laws was not necessarily going to help African Americans achieve social equality. Brown stated:

> The argument [of the plaintiff] also assumes that
> social prejudices may be overcome by legislation,
> and that equal rights cannot be secured to the negro

> except by an enforced commingling of the two races ...
> If the two races are to meet upon terms of social
> equality, it must be the result of natural affinities,
> a mutual appreciation of each other's merits, and a
> voluntary consent of individuals.

In other words, he thought social equality could only be achieved if the two races interacted with each other on their own terms. Since he did not believe laws would bring about this type of equality, he also did not feel the Separate Car Act created inequality. He felt Louisiana's law was reasonable. He also thought it was legal for a state to take action in the best interest of its citizens.

The Justices and Their Votes

Did Louisiana's law violate the Thirteenth Amendment?
  Yes: Harlan
  No: Brown, Field, Fuller, Gray, Peckman, Shiras, White
  No vote: Brewer

Is the Separate Car Act in violation of the equal protection and privileges and immunities clauses of the Fourteenth Amendment?
  Yes: Harlan
  No: Brown, Field, Fuller, Gray, Peckman, Shiras, White
  No vote: Brewer

The Lone Dissenter

Although nearly every justice sided with the majority, two did not join in the opinion. Justice David Brewer recused, or excused, himself. His daughter passed away, so he returned to his home in Leavenworth, Kansas. It is likely that Brewer would have dissented, or disagreed with, the majority opinion. His previous political and judicial decisions indicate that. However, Brewer was in Kansas and not present for the decision.

Justice Brewer recused himself because of his daughter's death.

The only official dissenter was Justice John Marshall Harlan. He was the same justice who had dissented in the court's ruling on the *Civil Rights Cases*. Harlan wrote a passionate opinion about the court's decision. The opinion also commented on segregation as a whole. In the years following the *Plessy* decision, the fears Harlan outlined in his opinion would come true. Specifically, he predicted the decades of oppression, or unfair treatment, that would result from the court's ruling in *Plessy*.

In his dissenting opinion, Harlan turned his attention first to the Thirteenth Amendment. Harlan did not believe the amendment only was meant to end slavery in the United States. He believed it should prevent "the imposition of any burdens or disabilities that constitute badges of slavery or servitude." In other words, he thought the amendment protected people from anything that limited their civil liberties. He felt segregation limited African Americans' civil liberties.

Harlan also argued that the Thirteenth Amendment was tied directly to the Fourteenth Amendment. He actually saw both amendments as inseparably linked. The Fourteenth Amendment provided "protection of the rights of those who had been" freed by the Thirteenth Amendment. This protection aimed to add to "the dignity and glory of American citizenship and to the security of personal liberty." For these reasons, Harlan did not agree with the other justices' belief that the case was not relevant to the Thirteenth Amendment.

Justice Harlan was an active critic of segregation.

Harlan's dissent then turned to the question of equality between races. He brought up the Reconstruction Amendments. Harlan believed that the Reconstruction Amendments were created to protect newly freed slaves. The amendments meant that African Americans could not be subjected to laws that denied them legal protections. In his view, the Louisiana law interfered with this protection.

Harlan even pointed out that the Separate Car Act only made a distinction between white and black citizens. The law made no reference to citizens of other nationalities or races. He argued that the law was designed specifically to discriminate against black people. He felt as though the law's true purpose was not to keep white people out of passenger cars for black people. He thought the law truly wanted to only exclude black people from the cars for white people. In this way, the law was created in order to not treat people equally.

Chief Justice Melville Fuller

Chief Justice Melville Fuller was appointed by President Grover Cleveland in 1888. According to his fellow justices, Fuller was a "skillful" manager of the court. He was able to "maintain collegiality," or a good relationship with his coworkers, during difficult cases. His legal attitude often reflected his belief in states' rights.

In his opinion in the case *In re Rahrer* (1891), Fuller argued that "the power of the state to impose restraints and burdens upon persons ... is a power originally and always belonging to the states." In other words, he believed the Constitution gave states this power. He did not believe the US government had the right to take this power away. This belief even extended to the Reconstruction Amendments. Fuller did not believe that the Fourteenth Amendment gave Congress the "power to legislate upon subjects which are within the domain of state legislation." In other words, he believed the US government had no business getting involved in state affairs.

These beliefs guided the way Fuller served as chief justice. These beliefs were central concepts to the majority opinion in the *Plessy* case.

Harlan also explained that the court's decision set a dangerous precedent. He wondered what would stop the state from racially segregating other facilities. He also wondered what would stop a state from segregating based on things other than race. For instance, he wondered if this precedent would give states permission to segregate based on religion.

Harlan also explained why racial segregation was so problematic. He argued that creating race-based laws went against the US Constitution. The Constitution had guaranteed everyone civil rights, regardless of race. He felt any laws that set up any sort of caste system based on race were unconstitutional. His argument concerning racial segregation became one of the most important dissents in American history. Harlan was making a case for complete equality under the law. This idea was not popular at the time. However, Harlan believed the Reconstruction Amendments made this position very clear.

Harlan concluded by discussing social equality. Unlike the majority, he thought laws could bring it about. Harlan argued that the government should "not permit seeds of race hate to be planted under the sanction of the law." In other words, he felt like segregation was a state's way of showing their distaste for a certain group of people. Harlan believed that this was wrong. He believed laws like Louisiana's only created more racial tension and inequality. He thought a "permanent peace" between races would be impossible without laws promoting integration, or the process of making public spaces available to all.

Harlan predicted segregation laws would forever brand former slaves and their descendants as second-class citizens. He believed segregation would create far more "evils" in America than integration. The legal inequalities throughout the late nineteenth and early twentieth century show how right Harlan was.

FIVE

The Impact of *Plessy*

In 1946, President Harry Truman established the President's Committee on Civil Rights. The committee was created to look at civil rights in America. The following year, the committee's report revealed the true effects of the *Plessy* decision. Between 1943 and 1944, 81 percent of lawsuits for job-based discrimination were filed on the basis of race. This was in comparison to 19 percent of lawsuits filed on the basis of religion, national origin, and immigration status. Ninety-seven percent of those complaints concerning job-based discrimination on the basis of race were made by African Americans. The report also showed that the unemployment rate in nearly every major city in America was more than double for African Americans what it was for white Americans. Federal Bureau of Investigation Director J. Edgar Hoover also commented that "it was seldom that a Negro man or woman was incarcerated who was not given a severe beating." In other words, African Americans were almost always beaten in jail. Additionally, the lynching, or a group practice of killing someone, of African Americans had increased dramatically since the late 1800s.

The report showed the terrible consequences of the *Plessy* ruling despite the efforts of many people to promote racial equality in the late nineteenth century. Booker T. Washington was a key part of this movement for equality. He was a leader

President Truman's Committee on Civil Rights found that 81 percent of claims of workplace discrimination were related to racial prejudice.

of African American communities in the South. A year before the *Plessy* decision, he stated that "in all things that are purely social we can be as separate as the fingers, yet one as the hand in all things essential to mutual progress." In other words, Washington thought that social segregation was acceptable. However, he believed people had to come together in order for the country to move forward.

W. E. B. Du Bois was also a civil rights activist. He understood Washington's arguments. However, he had his own opinions about progress. In 1903, he published his "Of Mr. Booker T. Washington and Others" essay in *The Souls of Black Folk*. In the essay, he argued that African Americans needed "first, political power, second, insistence on civil rights, third, higher education of Negro youth." In other words, Du Bois believed that African Americans needed education and political freedom. Du Bois believed that activism and

Racial Segregation:
Plessy v. Ferguson

Booker T. Washington became an early civil rights activist following the Civil War.

legal challenges were the only ways African Americans would achieve equality.

Du Bois pointed out that states had participated in "the disfranchisement of the Negro [and] the legal creation of a distinct status of civil inferiority for the Negro" since the 1880s. In other words, states had passed laws like Louisiana's Separate Car Act. These types of laws led to African Americans being robbed of certain privileges.

Du Bois was interested in protecting these privileges. He would go on to found the National Association for the Advancement of Colored People (NAACP). The association was founded to end all race-based discrimination and secure equal rights for African Americans. In the 1950s, the NAACP would help undo the *Plessy* ruling.

W. E. B. Du Bois argued that African Americans needed educational and political opportunities in order to see their rights protected.

Ida B. Wells-Barnett was another activist around this time. She was also a journalist and editor. She thought laws were not the only obstacles to equality. Racial violence was a problem throughout the nation. Wells-Barnett spoke of an

Wells-Barnett brought attention to the horrors of lynching.

"unwritten law" among white people that aimed to prevent equality. White Americans were angry about the new rights African Americans had. Their anger took the form of violence. White Americans would beat and kill African Americans. Wells-Barnett believed that these lynchings had to be stopped.

In the 1950s and 1960s, Martin Luther King Jr., Malcolm X, and other leaders of the civil rights movement would continue to struggle against the legacy of *Plessy*. The legalization of segregation had led to racial inequality. In schools, public facilities, voting booths, and private businesses, black Americans were subjected to a "badge of inferiority."

The Supreme Court and Civil Rights

Despite the effects of the *Plessy* decision, Homer Plessy's bravery was the same sort of bravery that civil rights activists had in the 1950s and 1960s. Plessy was a critic of segregation. He faced prison and public hatred for his decision to protest Louisiana's law. The Comité des Citoyens, the editors and writers of the *Crusader*, and all who worked on Plessy's case refused to allow African Americans to be treated like second-class citizens. Another generation and group of activists would have a similar spirit. They would even use the same amendment to make their case for the end of segregation.

The Historical Importance of *Plessy*

The court's ruling in *Plessy v. Ferguson* made segregation legal. The decision affected African Americans for decades. Historians tend to see *Plessy* as the court's refusal to protect racial equality. Indeed, the ruling in *Plessy* helped solidify many historical prejudices. In 1898, South Carolina's *News and Courier* mocked the decision. As a joke, it asked for segregated boats, saloons, restaurants, juries, Bibles, tax offices, and counties. However, this playful piece shed light on the effects of the *Plessy* decision. What seemed ridiculous actually became legal in many places.

The court's ruling did more than just provide a legal basis for segregation. In some ways, it also supported "seeds of hate" against black people. To this day, racism causes African Americans to experience brutality, violence, and oppression. In 2016, the Center for Policing Equity released a report. The report confirmed that African Americans were three times more likely to be victims of police brutality than white Americans. These cultural biases have their origins in the enslavement African Americans experienced. However, they also have important roots in the legacy of *Plessy*.

Racial Segregation:
Plessy v. Ferguson

Desegregation, or the end of segregation, was a slow process. However, most of the progress involved the Fourteenth Amendment. In cases like *Gitlow v. New York* (1925) and *Near v. Minnesota* (1931), the Supreme Court ruled that the states had to stand by the Bill of Rights and the rights secured to all American citizens by the Fourteenth Amendment. As a result, the court began to consider any violation of national liberties and rights by the states as unconstitutional. This idea was called the incorporation doctrine. It meant that all of an individual's federal rights had to be recognized by a state. The due process clause of the Fourteenth Amendment requires fair treatment by the law for all. This means states have to treat everyone fairly under the law no matter what. The incorporation doctrine became important to the struggle to end segregation.

In 1954, the NAACP hoped to use this new doctrine to help win the *Brown v. Board of Education of Topeka* case. This US Supreme Court case focused on whether or not the segregation of public schools was unconstitutional. In this case, Thurgood Marshall was the NAACP's main attorney. He argued that segregated schools were a violation of the Fourteenth Amendment's equal protection clause. All of the Supreme Court justices agreed. This ruling had significant effects. It challenged all forms of segregation. Specifically, this *Brown v. Board of Education* decision overturned the "separate but equal" precedent established by the *Plessy v. Ferguson* ruling.

In 1964, the United States Congress passed the Civil Rights Act. The act made discrimination on the basis of race, gender, color, national origin, or religion illegal. This act led to many other court decisions. In 1966, the Supreme Court declared certain voting requirements were unconstitutional.

Thurgood Marshall (*center*), George Hayes (*left*), and James Nabrit (*right*) pose for a picture after the *Brown v. Board of Education* verdict.

In 1978, the court supported the use of affirmative action programs. These were programs that provided opportunities to groups of people that were historically discriminated against.

Looking at Harlan's Dissent Again

After arguing the *Brown v. Board of Education* case, Thurgood Marshall would go on to serve as the first African American solicitor general of the United States. He would then become the first black justice on the Supreme Court. Marshall promoted the end of discrimination in all forms during his entire career.

Racial Segregation:
Plessy v. Ferguson

In 1993, Marshall's former colleague Constance Baker Motley said that "Marshall admired the courage of [John Marshall] Harlan more than any justice who has ever sat on the Supreme Court." Marshall thought Harlan's 1896 dissenting opinion in the *Plessy* case was brave. Marshall had actually mentioned Harlan's dissenting opinion in his *Brown v. Board of Education* arguments. Harlan made statements in support of equality that were very unpopular in the United States at the time. Marshall admired his bravery. Harlan's grandson, also named John Marshall Harlan, actually served alongside Marshall on the Supreme Court for several years.

The elder John Marshall Harlan was far from perfect. He owned slaves at one point in his life. He did not originally support the Thirteenth Amendment. Eventually, he changed his mind. He became a defender of the Republicans' Reconstruction agenda. However, his stances in race-related cases cost him. He was criticized by his peers. He was attacked in the press. His reputation also suffered because people thought his positions were inconsistent. Even still, Harlan's dissent directly inspired those responsible for ending segregation in the United States.

Although the ruling in *Plessy* paved the way for decades of segregation, the activism of Homer Plessy and the dissent of John Marshall Harlan also made history. Both of these men helped to undo generations of legalized racism.

Chronology

1857 The US Supreme Court rules that no black person is a citizen of the United States and that the federal government cannot regulate slavery without a constitutional amendment (*Dred Scott v. Sandford*).

1873 The Supreme Court establishes a narrow interpretation of the Fourteenth Amendment, stripping it of much of its power to protect minorities' rights (*Slaughterhouse Cases*).

1883 The Supreme Court rules that the Civil Rights Act of 1875 is unconstitutional (*Civil Rights Cases*).

1896 The Supreme Court rules that segregation of public facilities is constitutional, as long as equal accommodations are provided (*Plessy v. Ferguson*).

1938 The Supreme Court rules that states must provide in-state education opportunities for black and white students, though the schools can be segregated (*Missouri ex rel. Gaines v. Canada*).

1954 The Supreme Court rules that the use of separate educational institutions for students of different races is unconstitutional, effectively ending segregation (*Brown v. Board of Education of Topeka*).

1957 The government passes an act to enforce the
Brown v. Board decision and the integration of schools.

1964 The Civil Rights Act of 1964 bans discrimination
on the basis of race, gender, national origin, color,
or religion.

1965 Congress passes the Voting Rights Act, which
allows the government to protect all American citizens'
rights to vote.

1978 The Supreme Court rules that affirmative action
programs that use race as one of many factors in hiring
or accepting applicants are constitutional (*Regents of the
University of California v. Bakke*).

Glossary

abolish To formally end something.

appeal The act of asking a higher court to review and overturn a lower court's legal decision.

black codes Laws passed by Southern states after the Civil War that kept African Americans from exercising newly achieved freedoms during the Reconstruction Era.

brief A statement or summary of legal facts and points.

Civil Rights Act of 1866 A law that declared that every person born in the United States is a citizen, regardless of previous servitude, race, or color.

Civil Rights Act of 1875 A law that allowed the federal government to protect citizens' rights and provided those citizens equal treatment under the law.

desegregation The end of separating people based on race.

discrimination The process of treating an individual differently based on elements of his or her identity, such as race.

doctrine An established government policy.

Racial Segregation:
Plessy v. Ferguson

due process clause A part of the Fourteenth Amendment to the Constitution that requires that American citizens receive fair treatment by the judicial system.

equal protection clause A part of the Fourteenth Amendment to the Constitution that mandates American citizens are treated equally under the law.

incorporation doctrine The legal philosophy that states must respect citizens' rights as outlined in the Bill of Rights and the Constitution.

integration The process of making all public facilities and resources available to all races.

Jim Crow An insulting term for African Americans, and a term for state laws that enforced segregation based on race.

opinion A formal statement about a court's decision.

precedent A previous legal decision that is used to make future legal decisions.

segregation The legal separation of people based on race in public facilities and settings.

"separate but equal" doctrine The legal philosophy that allowed states to segregate public facilities so long as they provided separate and similar facilities for both groups of people.

sharecropper A farmer who rents land from a landowner. The farmer pays his or her rent with some of his or her crops.

Further Information

Books

Cates, David. *Plessy v. Ferguson: Segregation and the Separate but Equal Policy*. North Mankato, MN: Essential Library, 2012.

Hussey, Maria, ed. *The Rise of the Jim Crow Era*. New York: Britannica Educational Publishing, 2016.

Rubin, Sarah Goldman. *Brown v. Board of Education: A Fight for Simple Justice*. New York: Holiday House, 2016.

Torres, John A., and Sarah Betsy Fuller. *Desegregating Schools: Brown v. Board of Education*. New York: Enslow Publishing, 2017.

Websites

Landmark Cases of the US Supreme Court
http://landmarkcases.org/en/landmark

This website offers resources about major legal issues throughout US history.

Teaching American History

http://teachingamericanhistory.org

This site provides primary and secondary resources for students to examine important legal moments in American history.

Thirteen: The Supreme Court

https://www.thirteen.org/wnet/supremecourt/index.html

This website provides resources, readings, interactive opportunities, and lessons on major issues of Supreme Court history.

Videos

Brown v. Board of Education (1954): Separate Is NOT Equal

https://www.youtube.com/watch?v=aX9Dmo24_cc

This video provides an overview of the *Brown v. Board of Education of Topeka* case.

Plessy v. Ferguson

https://www.c-span.org/video/?86713-1/plessy-v-ferguson

In this video, Supreme Court Justice Clarence Thomas discusses the *Plessy v. Ferguson* decision.

Plessy v. Ferguson: Separate but Equal OK'd by High Court!

https://www.youtube.com/watch?v=Ldd0PLPG3E0

This video provides an overview of the *Plessy v. Ferguson* case.

Selected Bibliography

"Albion Winegar Tourgée." *Dictionary of North Carolina Biography*. Edited by William S. Powell. Chapel Hill: The University of North Carolina Press, 1996.

Blight, David W. *Race and Reunion: The Civil War in American Memory*. Cambridge, MA: The Belknap Press of Harvard University Press, 2001.

"The Civil Rights Cases." The Legal Information Institute, October 16, 1883. https://www.law.cornell.edu/supremecourt/text/109/3.

Douglass, Frederick. "Frederick Douglass on Jim Crow." The Gilder Lehrman Institute of American History: History Now. Accessed December 12, 2017. https://www.gilderlehrman.org/content/frederick-douglass-jim-crow-1887.

Fireside, Harvey. *Separate and Unequal: Homer Plessy and the Supreme Court Decision That Legalized Racism.* New York: Carroll & Graf Publishers, 2004.

Goldstene, Claire. *The Struggle for America's Promise: Equal Opportunity at the Dawn of Corporate Capital.* Jackson: University Press of Mississippi, 2014.

Racial Segregation:
Plessy v. Ferguson

Hall, Kermit, ed. *American Legal History: Cases and Materials.* 5th ed. New York: Oxford University Press, 2017.

Hoffer, Williamjames Hull. *Plessy v. Ferguson: Race and Inequality in Jim Crow America.* Lawrence: University Press of Kansas, 2012.

"The Law Is Constitutional." *Roanoke Daily Times*, May 19, 1896. https://chroniclingamerica.loc.gov/lccn/sn95079481/1896-05-19/ed-1/seq-1.

Medley, Keith W. "Plessy v. Ferguson: The Organizing History of the Case." Teaching a People's History: Zinn Education. Accessed December 12, 2017. https://zinnedproject.org/materials/plessy-v-ferguson.

Mills, Nicolaus. "Racism's Triumph on the Supreme Court: *Plessy v. Ferguson* Turns 120." *Daily Beast*, February 26, 2016. https://www.thedailybeast.com/racisms-triumph-on-the-supreme-court-plessy-v-ferguson-turns-120.

"Plessy v. Ferguson." Oyez. Accessed December 12, 2017. https://www.oyez.org/cases/1850-1900/163us537.

"Separate Cars for the Races." *Weekly Messenger*, May 23, 1896. https://chroniclingamerica.loc.gov/lccn/sn88064454/1896-05-23/ed-1/seq-1.

"Supreme Court Decides the 'Jim Crow' Car Law is Constitutional." *New Ulm Review*, May 20, 1896. https://chroniclingamerica.loc.gov/lccn/sn89081128/1896-05-20/ed-1/seq-2.

Thompson, Charles. "Harlan's Great Dissent." *Kentucky Humanities* 1. Lexington: Kentucky Humanities Council, 1996.

Williams, Timothy. "Study Supports Suspicion That Police Are More Likely to Use Force on Blacks." *New York Times*, July 7, 2016. https://www.nytimes.com/2016/07/08/us/study-supports-suspicion-that-police-use-of-force-is-more-likely-for-blacks.html?_r=1.

Woodward, C. Vann. "The Case of the Louisiana Traveler." In *Quarrels That Have Shaped the Constitution*, edited by John A. Garrity. New York: Harper and Row Publishers, Inc., 1987.

Index

About the Author

Zachary Deibel is a social studies instructor at Cristo Rey Columbus High School in Columbus, Ohio. He holds a BA in history from American University and an MA in history from Arkansas State University. He enjoys reading, writing, and thinking about American history, government, and society with his students.